Dehydrator cookbook :

THE COMPLETE GUIDE TO DEHYDRATING FOOD

Foreword

Although the process of dehydrating food is as old as the world, many of us have never heard of this practice. And just as many people have no idea that such a thing as a food dehydrator even exists. However, and as you probably already know if you are holding this book, dehydrating food is at the same time healthy, cost saving and smart.

Should you be a sportsperson seeking nutritional benefits, a mother wanting to diversify her cooking in a healthy and cost saving way, or just a great fan of dried fruit and vegetables, surely you will find what you are looking for with a food dehydrator.

It must be said that this appliance proves very useful to cook dried fruit or vegetables, but also to dry meat or even to preserve your food longer.

In this book you are going to become familiar with all the tips to use a food dehydrator in the best possible conditions, from choosing your dehydrator to processing your food, and tips to store your dehydrated foods.

If food dehydration remains a mystery to you, it is high time you solve that mystery!

Chapter 1: What is a food dehydrator?

I. What is a food dehydrator ?

How about we start from scratch, to make sure everyone keeps up? Before you become an expert on food dehydration, it seems interesting to thoroughly study this principle, and the leading appliance among dehydrated food enthusiasts: the food dehydrator.

1. Introducing the food dehydrator

Behind intricate looks, the food dehydrator is nothing more than an appliance equipped with an electric resistor and a fan. As its name states, this appliance allows you to dehydrate food products (fruit, vegetables, meat, fish, etc.) thanks to its capacity to heat products at a low temperature.

This household appliance is therefore ideal if you are truly enthusiastic about dried fruit and vegetables. It is also very practical to keep your products longer (especially if you own a vegetable patch or many fruit trees).

Indeed, it is the water contained in the food that make microorganisms and bacteria flourish. Once the water is gone, foods can be kept much longer.

The dehydrator is made up of a box that heats and blows air to the desired temperature and circulates it between the various levels (also called «trays») of the appliance. Food products are finely sliced and arranged flat on the trays. Thanks to the ambient hot air, the water contained in the foods is going to slowly evaporate. In a nutshell: they dry.

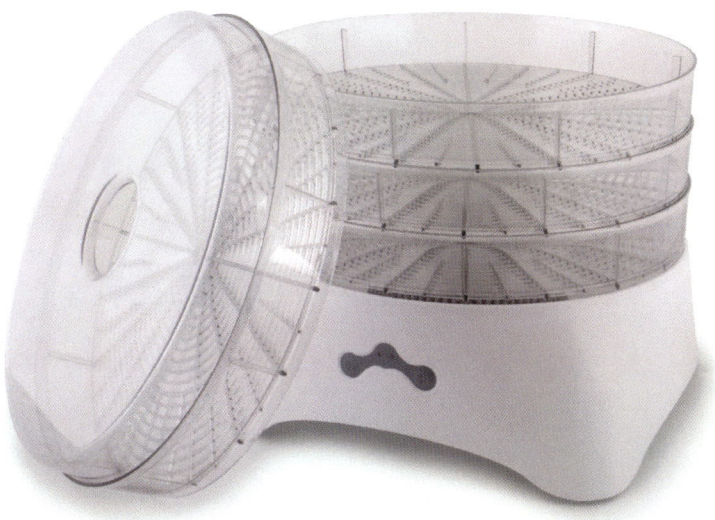

2. Food dehydration through the ages

Drying the food to keep it longer is as old as the world. Let it be said that we did not wait for the food dehydrator or electricity to show up to do it: the sun was doing the job just fine (but in a less practical and quick way!).

As early as Antiquity, food was already being dehydrated to keep the perishable products longer. The products were left to dry out in the sun for hours, flat on a stone, to be stored for a long time, to benefit from the harvests longer.

During long journeys, seafarers would take dried foods on their ships, to make up for the lack of fresh produce, which allowed explorers to venture further and further out while discovering the oceans.

Thanks to technical progress, food dehydration has become much faster and more efficient, and still allows us to store food longer.

Let's also admit that food dehydration is also used out of sheer preference: dried fruit and veggies are perfect snacks!

3. The principle of dehydrating food

Dehydrating food means drying out the water occurring naturally in all food. There are three stages:

- First, you have to slice the foods finely, so they can dry more easily. Then you arrange them in the dehydrator.
- Next, they are going to let go of the liquid they have, due to them being exposed for a long time to a limited heat (under 60 °C / 140 °F for fruit and vegetables).
- Once the water has dried out completely, the food products can be stored in airtight jars (dried food must absolutely be stored away from humidity).

This way of preparing food has many advantages. Since microbes and bacteria have been removed, these products will not rot and will be edible much longer. Since they shrink while drying, the products take up less space and are therefore easier to store. Thanks to a limited cooking temperature, ingredients keep their enzymes, vitamins and minerals. So, they remain very healthy.

Dehydration is hence economic regarding storage and budget, since it allows you to buy and keep large quantities of food. From a nutritional point of view, dried food products often retain more value than cooked products.

4. Assets of the food dehydrator

Although it is not the most wide-spread household appliance (most households don't even know it exists!), the food dehydrator still offers multiple positive features. The food dehydrator is a kitchen appliance that is both practical and unobtrusive, and advantageous.

For a start, it is an absolute must-have for anyone who wants to dehydrate their food. Indeed, the food dehydrator is the only appliance that can heat the food at a temperature low enough to dry it without burning it.

It is a perfect device to keep fruit and vegetables for longer. If you buy your food products in bulk or if you grow fruit and vegetables, the dehydrator will allow you to store them year-round. Not only will you stop wasting, but you will also be able to enjoy your favorite food out of season.

The dehydrator is otherwise a multipurpose equipment. It allows you to prepare dried fruit, dried meat and fish, cereal bars, herbal tea, vegetable chips, and so on. Enough to sustain sportspeople, foodies, chefs...and kids who object to eating up their veggies!

It is also an environmentally-friendly and budget-friendly appliance if you are a dried fruit or vegetables enthusiast. Environmentally-friendly, since using it allows you to prepare local fruit and vegetables, thus limiting transport and packaging compared to buying dried fruit and vegetables in supermarkets. And budget-friendly, since dehydrating your food yourself costs less than buying it already dried.

Finally, this device allows you to prepare healthier dried vegetables and fruit. Indeed, you can decide to only pick organic fruit and vegetables, so you are certain your dried food has never been treated (preservatives, added sugar, etc).

5. The Benefits of dehydrated food products

In many cases (and maybe in yours!), people turn to food dehydration because they want to improve their diet. And that's far from being a bad idea!

In fact, it must be said that dried food can be a real health benefit nutrition-wise. So, it is always a good idea to give it a closer look when studying food dehydrating.

5. THE BENEFITS OF DEHYDRATED FOOD PRODUCTS

What do dried fruit and vegetables contain ?

The main advantage of investing in a food dehydrator is that this device allows you to «cook» your fruit and vegetables without taking away their core nutritional values.

Even if dehydration consists in removing the water contained in fruit, they will not lose their nutrients in the process.

So, do know that dried fruit and vegetables still contain vitamins, antioxidants, iron, magnesium, minerals, fiber or potassium. All of which are condensed in a mini portion, since your dried fruit or vegetable is naturally more compact than its fresh counterpart.

All these elements that can be found in dried fruit and vegetables help facilitate digestion, boost your immune system and keep you well any time of the year. It is even more enjoyable that dried food products are often easier to use than fresh products.

> **IMPORTANT NOTICE:** dried fruit still contain a high level of carbohydrates, which is why you will sometimes hear they are bad for your health. The truth is, dried fruit are a great source of energy, but it is important not to eat too many of them to avoid an excessive carbohydrate intake. You can eat them as snacks or mixed with other ingredients, but you should never eat dried fruit by the handful!

Dried fruit : a source of energy for sportspeople

It is no coincidence if more and more sportspeople are interested in food dehydration: dehydrated fruit is indeed the ideal snack for any sportsperson. And needless to say, using a food dehydrator will mean long-term savings compared to store-bought dried fruit!

Highly recommended for sportspeople, dried fruit help you get in shape and recharge your batteries during intense exercise. They can be eaten before, during and after the sport session to provide the body with the minerals it needs.

I. WHAT IS A FOOD DEHYDRATOR

Very light and non-obtrusive, dried fruit can be taken anywhere, including in a tracksuit pocket or a hiking backpack. They provide very appreciated carbohydrates during endurance activities (such as running, brisk walking, football…).

DEHYDRATED FOOD : EXCELLENT FOR THE DIGESTION

Most fruit and vegetables contain fibers which are entirely kept during the dehydrating process. Dehydrated foods also keep their enzymes, which make digestion much easier.

So, dried fruit and vegetables help with digestion and facilitate bowel functions. They help reducing abdominal cramps and constipation. You'll be able to eat them as dessert or mixed in your main courses, to help you digest your lunch.

DEHYDRATED FOOD : TO BOOST YOUR IMMUNE SYSTEM

Generally speaking, dehydrated fruit and vegetable help boosting your immune system as much as fresh fruit and vegetables. They also help you fight diseases and health risks:

- They help you fights osteoporosis (raisins),
- They prevent anaemia (dried figs),
- They help against constipation (prunes and dried mangoes),
- They help control weight,
- They help fight tiredness (dried dates),
- They strengten the bones and boost the immune system,
- They help reduce blood pressure (dried apricots).

You get it, dehydrated foods are worth just as much as fresh foods. And if they reconcile you with vegetables or replace less healthy snacks (like chips or candies), it's a double win!

6. Different ways of using the food dehydrator

Of course, the main usage of a food dehydrator will be to dehydrate fresh food products, but you should also keep in mind that you can cook creative recipes with it.

Indeed, with such an equipment you will be able to prepare many preparations:

- Dried fruit and vegetables,
- Fruit leather,
- Vegetable chips,
- Vegetable stock,
- Muesli,
- Cereal bars,
- Dried meat (it's even better if you marinate it first),
- Dried fish,
- Yogurts (if you can regulate the temperature precisely on your device), etc.

Although a dehydrator is bought first and foremost to prepare dried fruit and vegetables, it is quickly possible to multiply its uses and the recipes with it.

Don't worry, should you be interested, the fifth chapter of this book will provide you with many recipes and tips, to help you get the most out of your food dehydrator. But before that, we have many other things to talk about!

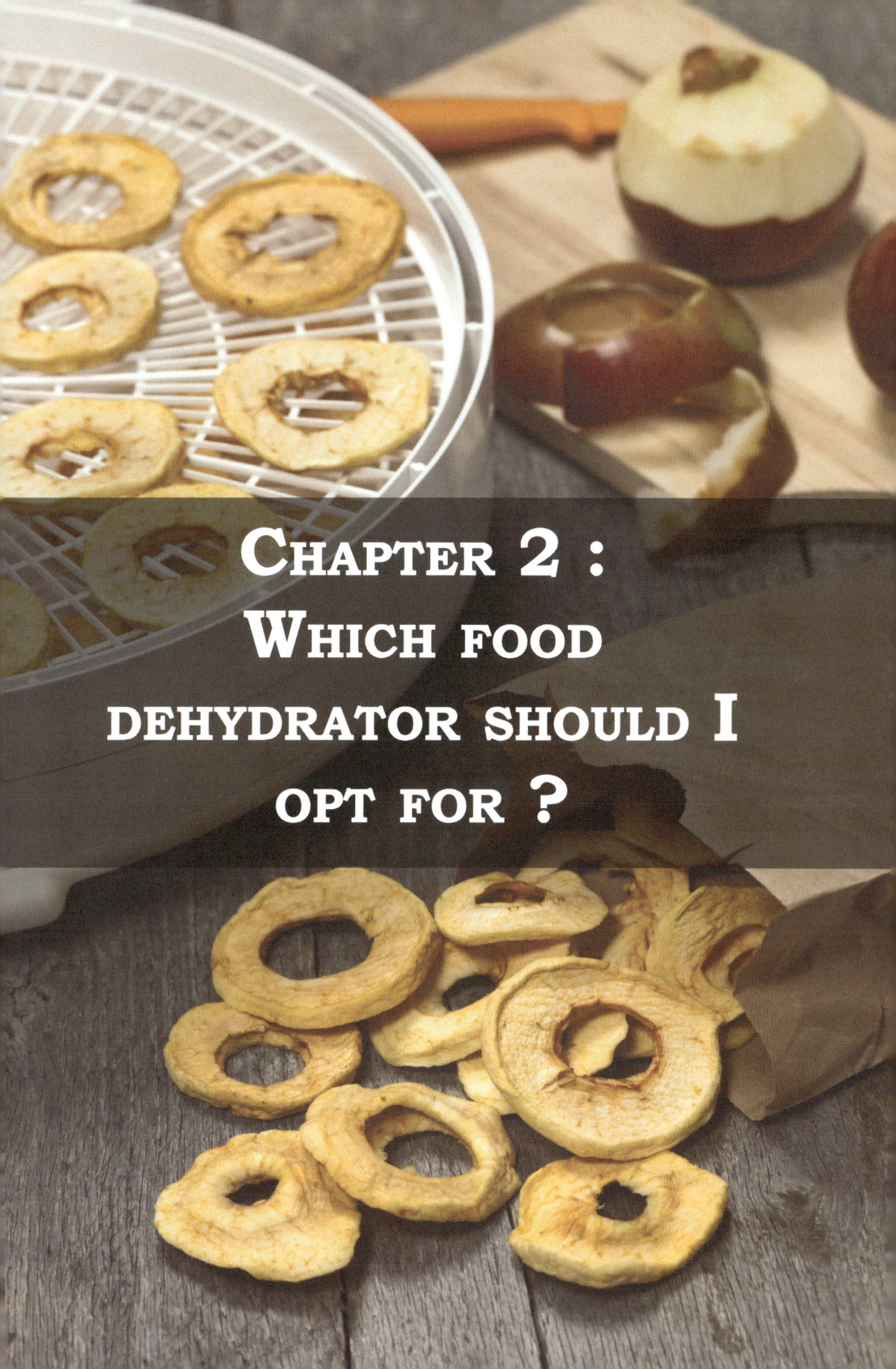

Chapter 2: Which food dehydrator should I opt for?

II. Which food dehydrator should I opt for ?

You now know everything about the benefits of dehydrated food. But to try it for yourself, it is important to get the right equipment!

It is never easy, as a beginner in food dehydrating, to choose your first food dehydrator. In fact, even though this appliance remains quite unknown to cooks, there still are many brands and many versions.

So, how do you make an enlightened choice? If you have yet to buy your equipment, this chapter will tell you all there is to know about the various dehydrators and will help you decide.

1. THE PRICE, AN IMPORTANT AND FLOATING FACTOR

It is always important to get some information on the price of a food dehydrator to start with. It is indeed good to know that the prices can range from a couple of dozen dollars to several hundreds.

The price for a food dehydrator will vary depending, first, on its shape:

- It will go from $50 to $370 on average for a vertical airflow (usually round or square shape).
- You will need at least $250 to $600 for a horizontal airflow (usually rectangular).

There are some very good models for $100 to $250. Beyond that price range, you will find high-capacity and upmarket dehydrators.

Entry-level products cost about $100. You might want to have a look at them! If you are new to the art of food dehydrating, and not quite sure you are going to use your dehydrator on a regular basis, buying a cheaper dehydrator is a good way of testing it out without spending a fortune.

Of course, you should always take time to compare functionalities and features for each product, to be sure you are making the right decision.

2. Electric or solar dryer ?

Before you buy anything, you have to decide on the type of dehydrator you are the most interested in. Most food dehydrators are electric, by far. Even though a food dehydrator does not use up too much energy, it does use some.

So, you might want to opt for a solar dryer, which uses the clean energy coming from the sun. But be careful: the two devices are far from identical.

Electric food dehydrators

As we have already mentioned, food dehydrating usually needs electricity. An electric food dryer will function thanks to an electric resistor, and must be turned on from 8 to 15 hours on average to dry the foods out.

But don't worry, the power for an electric food dehydrator is way inferior to the power for an oven (it is usually between 200 and 600 W, versus more than 1,500 W for a traditional oven), and the energy cost for such an appliance hardly ever goes over $1 an hour!

Even if the (very light) energy use of such an appliance can put off those willing to reduce their electricity costs, it is obvious that electric models have undeniable advantages.

Indeed, a food dehydrator can easily be used year-round, and can dehydrate most foods in less than 10 hours. These appliances can also accommodate impressive quantities of foods.

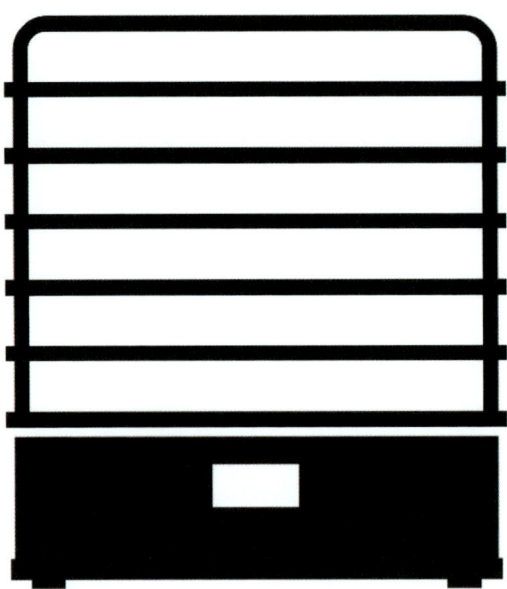

Solar food dehydrators

Of course, those of you who want to reduce their number of household appliances might favor an option that is more natural than the electric food dryer. They will find such an option in the solar dryer.

Just like the solar oven, the solar dryer is an appliance that does not use any electricity, and dehydrates food with the sun rays only. It is usually made up of a wooden box equipped with a steel or glass sheet that attracts sun heat and slowly cooks the foods without exposing them to the open air.

Even though this energy-free operation is tempting, it is also clear that a solar dryer will be a lot less efficient and quick than its electric counterpart. Moreover, no need to look for such a device if you don't live in a really sunny area.

You get it, for a use that is both more universal and multipurpose, we do recommend you buy an electric model.

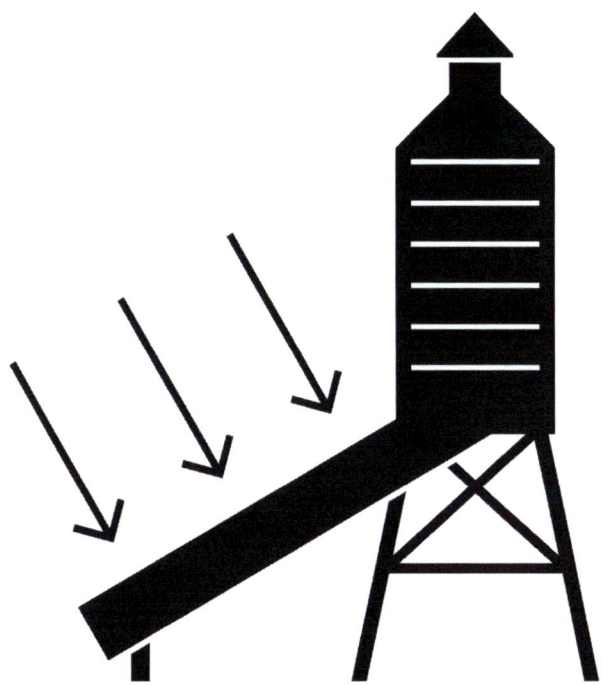

3. Vertical or horizontal airflow ?

It is one thing to choose an electric dehydrator, but it is another to decide on the category of electric dehydrator. There are two of them.

You will have to choose between a vertical airflow and a horizontal airflow.

The former is round and is usually divided in three trays (or more) piled up. The horizontal food dehydrator, for its part, is square with at least 5 trays, on which you can arrange your fruit, vegetables, meat and other foods.

Before you buy a food dehydrator, always check the following features regardless of its shape:

- Optimum capacity: should you live in a household of two or many more, it is always better to choose a large capacity. Dehydrators usually have 3 to 10 trays.
- A timer and thermostat that can be adjusted: these two settings are both key, since all foods do not necessarily dry at the same temperature and for the same length of time.

- Ease of use: if it is your first time using a dehydrator, make sure the model you will opt for is neither too technical, nor too specific. A model that is simpler and more functional suits beginners better.
- Easy cleaning: if you use it, you have to clean it. So, make sure the device of your choosing is easy to clean to save time and avoid damage due to the products used.

Once you have made sure these boxes are checked, you may choose either a vertical or horizontal equipment.

The vertical airflow food dehydrator

The vertical airflow food dehydrator is a compact device, usually with a round shape. It is perfect for occasional use. Its engine is located in its base, so the air is going to circulate from the bottom trays upwards.

This device can be equipped with several trays, allowing the dehydration of several types of foods at the same time. Its main advantages are its non-obtrusiveness, its low-noise and its reasonable price.

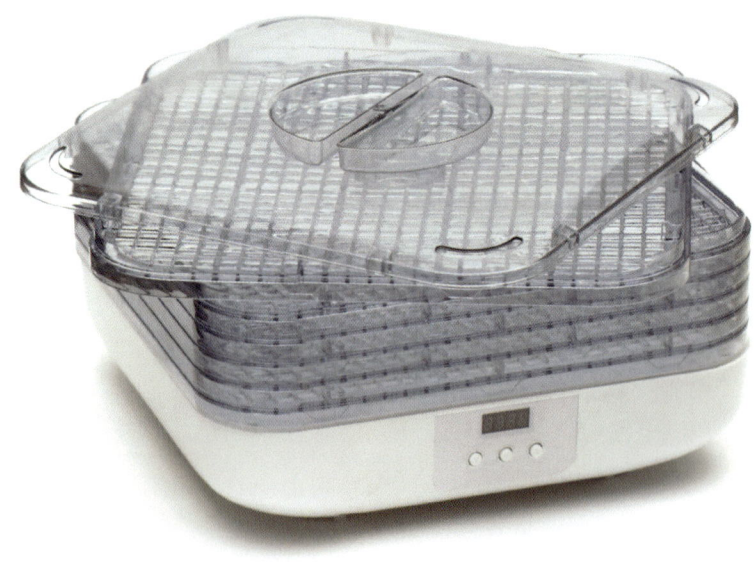

Why choose a vertical airflow ?

The vertical airflow is particularly advantageous because of its small dimensions. This is actually one of its main assets, since because of its shape, it usually takes up little space in the kitchen and can be put away easily. Indeed, its engine (located at the bottom of the equipment) can be separated from the trays.

Moreover, round-shaped dehydrators are quieter, which can be highly appreciated in the long term. Also, depending on the quantity of food you want to prepare, it is possible to increase or decrease the number of trays.

The main asset of the vertical airflow is its price, lower than a horizontal food dehydrator.

Which vertical airflow should I choose ?

You will find diverse models of vertical airflows on the market.

Depending on your expectations, some will prove better than others. Taking up little space, round dehydrators can hold about 3 to 10 trays. There are of course many brands.

The cost of vertical food dehydrators

The price of a dehydrator will vary from one model to the other depending on their features (number of trays, timer, adjustable thermostat, etc).

Vertical dehydrators are usually less expensive than the horizontal ones. Indeed, a vertical airflow will cost about $50. Some upmarket models can cost $180 and sometimes more. Such devices will rarely cost over $370 though.

THE HORIZONTAL AIRFLOW

The horizontal airflow is a kind of food dryer that is more elaborate and complex than the vertical one. Its engine is at the back of the device, so that the heat is equally dispatched among the trays.

The main advantage for this type of model is its capacity to evenly accommodate a larger quantity of foods (it can accommodate up to 10 trays, sometimes more depending on the models).

II. WHICH FOOD DEHYDRATOR SHOULD I OPT FOR

Consequently, this device will be favored by owners of restaurants or by «intensive» users of food dehydration, who are looking to process the largest possible quantity of foods.

Why choose a horizontal food dehydrator ?

The horizontal food dehydrator is often considered an upmarket product, more efficient than the vertical devices.

Horizontal dehydrators usually feature a thermostat and a timer, which allow you to master the dehydration of the food products better.

Moreover, the horizontal food dehydrator is wider. So, both for large families and food lovers, it is the best option, since you can dry a large quantity of food. Attention: it is in return more voluminous and harder to put away !

How much does a horizontal airflow cost ?

Horizontal dehydrators will not be your first choice if you are on a budget.

In fact, a horizontal airflow usually costs between $250 and $600.

So, you get it, choosing your dehydrator will depend on how you intend to use it. It might therefore be a good idea, if you are a beginner or if you are not quite sure to be using your food dehydrator on a regular basis, to start by buying a round-shaped equipment.

4. What size for my food dehydrator ?

When buying a new household appliance, the dimension issue must be considered. It must be said that the size of a food dehydrator will depend on its shape (horizontal airflow or vertical airflow).

As mentioned earlier, horizontal airflows are much larger and harder to store, since they are made up of one single piece. In turn, they accommodate a larger quantity of food.

Vertical airflows are by far easier to store, since you can absolutely separate the base from the trays.

Always remember that a food dehydrator is going to be running for long hours. If it is too large for your kitchen, it might be in your way when stored, but also while you are using it.

5. Other criteria to choose your device

You now know a lot on the various dehydrator options on the market. We still have to discuss the last criteria that can help you make your decision. Beside the size and type of model, the difference sometimes lays in details.

Featuring a timer, for example, is almost a must-have. The timer allows you to program the exact number of dehydration hours when drying food (operation time always depends on the kind of food, as we will see later). Once the number of hours is up, the appliance will be turned off automatically. Without a timer, you would have to keep an eye on the process all the time, in order not to wait for too long!

A thermostat is another key feature. The thermostat will allow you to regulate the cooking temperature, which will also vary depending on the type of food to dehydrate.

Another important detail you want to check: noise! Low range devices will tend to be loud, which might prove annoying if you live in a flat... or just if you like a quiet environment.

To conclude, the design, the sturdiness and the materials used can be your last criteria for choice. Whatever your choice, always remember that quality usually goes with the price. You can't expect too much from a 50-dollar-device...

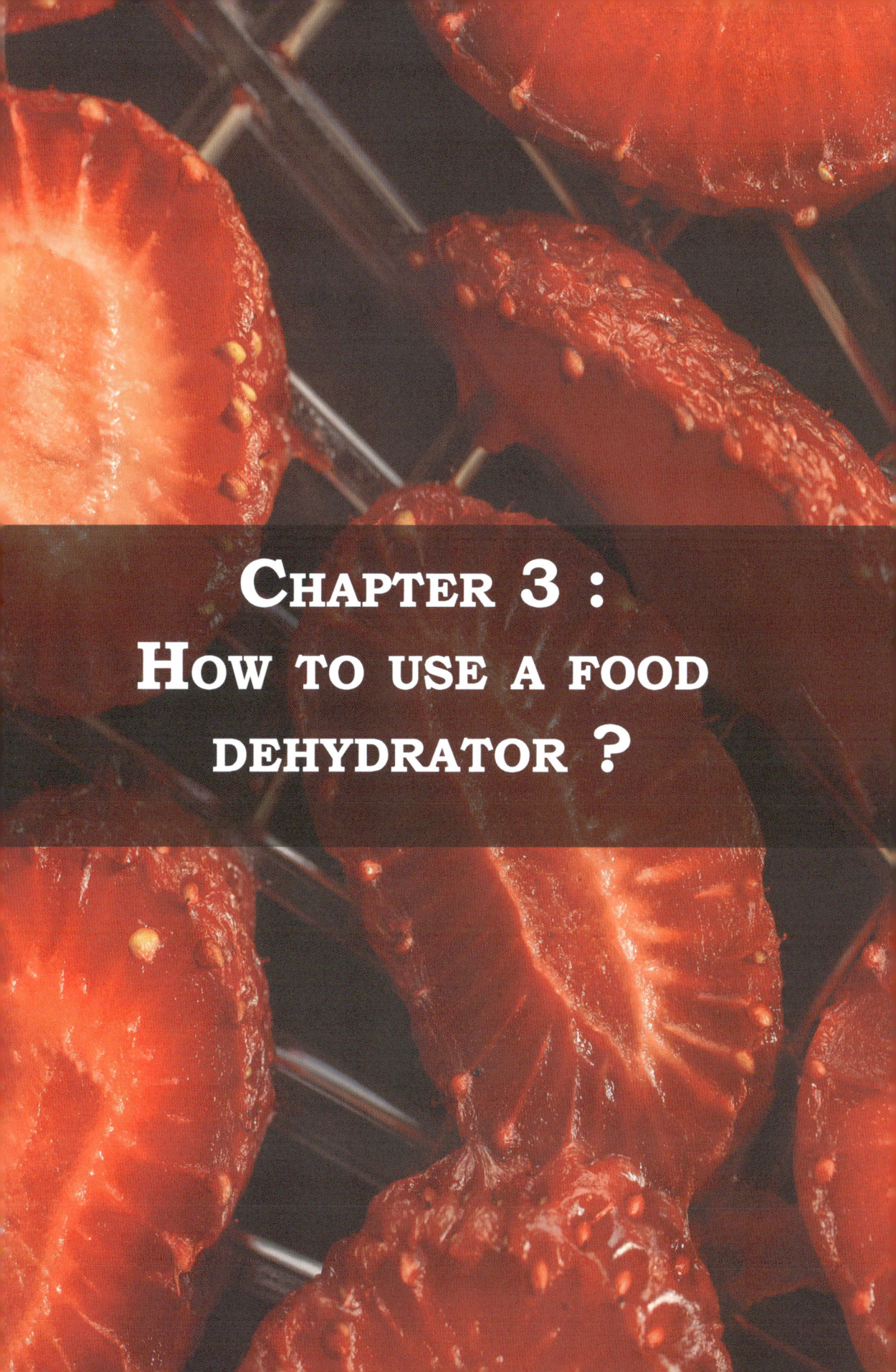

Chapter 3: How to use a food dehydrator?

III. How to use a food dehydrator ?

As we have already discussed at length, the food dehydrator enables you to dehydrate your own foods: vegetables, fruit, herbs, meat, fish... But to make the most of this household appliance, it is important to look carefully at its operation and its uses.

1. Operation of a food dehydrator

Don't worry, if you dread operating a food dehydrator, it is in the end rather easy to use. The most important thing is to understand quite well how it works, but also and mostly to know how to process the food prior to dehydrating it.

How to use a food dehydrator ?

Using a food dehydrator is usually basic, but it is good to get some information before trying a recipe in the dehydrator.

The basic principle of food dehydration

The main function of a dehydrator is to dehydrate fruit and vegetables. So, you simply have to quickly prepare your food before dehydrating it to be assured of a good-quality result.

Let's go together through the necessary stages to dehydrate fruit and vegetables.

First, it is important to thoroughly clean both your foods and your working area, to remove any bacteria. Ideally, you should wear a pair of gloves so as not to soil the food while processing it.

The foods must then be finely and evenly sliced, with a slicer, so the process of dehydration goes faster and is uniform. Arrange the slices of food on the various trays of your dehydrator. The slices must neither be on top of each other, nor prevent the air from circulating. If one tray is full, use another one. Once the trays are ready, close the lid of the dehydrator.

The next stage is to connect your appliance to an electric plug and to turn it on. Depending on the model, you might have to set the thermostat and the timer. The first one is to set the temperature, and the other one to set the dehydration duration. Both will vary depending on the food being dehydrated. Fruit for example should be dried at a temperature between 57°C/134°F for 3 to 12 hours depending on the fruit (and its humidity rate).

If you are equipped with a vertical airflow, it could be appropriate to switch trays from time to time during the drying process, because food products on the top trays may take longer to dry out completely.

To be noted that each model of food dehydrator is delivered with instructions, which will take you through the operation secrets in details!

> **PROCESSING THE FRUIT AND VEGETABLES TO BE DEHYDRATED:** if it is not systematic, some foods can be slightly processed prior to dehydration. For example, it is recommended to soak fruit for a few minutes (except berries) in a mix of 1/4 lemon juice and 3/4 water. Vegetables in turn can be quickly steamed or boiled. These steps allow your foods to keep a nice color, and their nutritional values.

Cooking with the dehydrator

Your food dehydrator also allows you to cook some recipes, including herbal teas or snacks.

As one might suspect, it would be too easy to just lay the products as they are in a dehydrator to enjoy delicious beef jerky, fruit leather or muesli.

It is therefore very common to have to cook before or after dehydrating the foods, to prepare unique and original recipes.

Later in this book, we will detail the various recipes and tips to prepare them and get the most out of your food dryer.

How does the process of dehydration work ?

As with a conventional oven, the food dehydrator is made up of a heating component (usually an electric resistor). But in contrast with the oven, the food dryer is also equipped with a fan, which makes the heat circulate between several trays. It is precisely this fan that makes the device noisy.

This combination makes the food products dry in a few hours, through a slow and moderate cooking, which is going to dry out the foods without burning them.

A dehydrator uses a lot less energy than a conventional oven, since it is a lot less powerful (otherwise, foods would be burnt before they get dehydrated!)

2. What is a food dehydrator made up of ?

To use your food dehydrator in the best way, it seems useful to give you some information on its build. If the instructions for the device certainly give you precious information on each part of the device, let us tell you more.

A food dehydrator is systematically made up of various elements, that ensure its proper functioning:

- An electric resistor: the engine of the dehydrator is equipped with an electric resistor, namely a kind of steel spring that heats up with electricity.

- A fan: still in the engine, a fan makes the warm air circulate throughout the device.

- Trays: the compartments are commonly called trays (each tray allows you to arrange your foods in slices) and are located in what is called the cage of the device.

- A lid: a dehydrator is equipped with a lid, which maintains an even temperature throughout the dehydration process and prevents heat losses.

- A thermostat: depending on the model, some might be equipped with a thermostat, so that you can regulate the temperature depending on the food you want to dry.

- A timer: another optional feature, the timer allows you to turn the device on and off, even when you are away. It is sometimes key, since dehydrating products can take up to several hours, and you might not be available when it is time to end the process!

Apart from the trays and the lid (removable), these various parts are all contained in a box, usually made up of plastic.

If you opt for a vertical airflow dehydrator, trays will pile up on top of each other, and you will have to put the lid on top of the pile of trays.

If you opt for a horizontal airflow dehydrator, the trays slide into the appliance, and the lid is a door that shuts the equipment.

III. HOW TO USE A FOOD DEHYDRATOR

> **CLEANING TIPS FOR THE TRAYS:** to prevent the food from sticking to the trays too much, you can use greaseproof paper or non-stick sheets. Spraying vegetable oil on the trays can also help. If despite these measures your food sticks, we recommend soaking the trays in very hot water, with mild detergent (washing-up liquid) and using a toothbrush to remove the small bits, if necessary.

3. CHOOSING YOUR FRUIT AND VEGETABLES : OUR TIPS

As often when following a recipe, a successful outcome can partly depend on the quality of the chosen ingredients. And it is all the more important when you decide to dehydrate fruit and vegetables.

Here are a few tips to select the best products at the best price:

PREFER FRESH PRODUCE

Even if it is possible to dehydrate frozen fruit and vegetable, it is of course better to work with fresh food. Indeed, fresh fruit and vegetables have a higher nutritional value, and will be easier to prepare.

3. CHOOSING YOUR FRUIT AND VEGETABLES : OUR TIPS

Make seasonal fruit and vegetables your first choice, they will be a lot cheaper and easier to find. Opting for seasonal products is actually usually more environmentally friendly, since your products will not have travelled across the globe to get onto your plate! A seasonality table is attached to this book as an appendix, to help you choose what fruit or vegetable to buy for each time of the year.

If you have a large food dryer, don't hesitate to buy your vegetables in large quantities, this might mean you will pay less for them.

Of course, your piece of fruit or vegetable should still be fresh before dehydration, you should never use ingredients that are moldy or way too damaged. The best way is to buy your produce in the morning, to prepare them in the afternoon.

On the other hand, feel free to work with fruit and vegetables that are slightly damaged or don't look very nice. The flaws that show on the piece of fruit will no longer show once it is sliced and dehydrated!

III. HOW TO USE A FOOD DEHYDRATOR

> **BUDGET TIP:** always go for damaged or too ripe produce if they are on sale. Sometimes producers offer a bargain for damaged fruit and vegetables, or sell them in bulks. You will just have to process them as soon as you get home, and you can pride yourself on a good deal for the ingredients you have dehydrated.

Always go for organic when you can

Be it to dehydrate food or not, we suggest you always prefer organic fruit and vegetables. This way, you can safely keep the peel when dehydrating, and be sure to have perfectly healthy ingredients.

Indeed, non-organic foods are usually heavily processed, and may retain chemical residues that cooking will not necessarily remove. It is also considered that organic fruit and vegetables contain more vitamins and antioxidants minerals.

If you don't buy organic ingredients, remember to thoroughly wash your fruit and vegetables before processing them, and we advise you peel them.

Eat local

If you are considering dehydrating large quantities of fruit and vegetables, it is important to find a reliable producer.

To find the best ingredients at the best price, it is best to look for fruit and vegetables that are both organic AND local.

You often find local producers that offer direct sale for their fruit and vegetables. This way, you benefit from the best prices, and you can even offer the producer to «get rid» of their damaged products for a modest sum!

It is really important to find local producers if you throw yourself into food dehydration, because this will enable you to work with best quality products for a better price than at the supermarket.

4. How to dehydrate fruit and vegetables ?

Once you have correctly selected your fruit and vegetables, it is crucial to carefully prepare them. Let's go through useful tips to be sure to get delicious dried fruit and vegetables.

Slice the ingredients well

The finer the slices, the easier the dehydration process. Once your ingredients are carefully washed, it is time to chop or finely slice them.

To do so, make sure you have well-cutting tools like a sharp knife or a slicer, so the slices are even. Be careful to cut even slices, otherwise all the pieces of fruit and vegetables will not be ready at the same time.

Please note that small fruit (strawberries, raspberries, etc.) do not necessarily need cutting. But still care to open them slightly lengthwise, to prevent the skin from drying out completely before the inside of the fruit is dehydrated.

Once your food is sliced and ready, proceed to cooking them quickly. The quicker your fresh foods are processed, the longer they will retain their taste and nutrients.

> **IMPORTANT NOTICE:** if your fruit and vegetables are not organic, prefer peeling them, since the peel might retain some pesticides, even after washing them.

Should I keep the peel?

It is perfectly logical to wonder whether to keep the peel of the fruit and vegetables when dehydrating them. And the answer will vary depending on the food.

There is thankfully one simple rule: if you can eat the peel of the fresh ingredient, then you can eat it too when it is dehydrated. On the contrary, if the peel of the fruit or vegetable cannot be eaten fresh, then you have to peel it.

In all logic, you can keep the peel for apples, pears, potatoes or apricots. On the contrary, you will have to peel bananas, mangoes or kiwis.

It is possible to keep the rind of citrus fruit, keeping in mind it will make them a bit sour.

If you keep the peel or rind of your food, arrange the food peel down, since it will tend to stick less than the flesh. This will also prevent the pulp of the fruit or vegetable from running down on the trays below.

Please note that the skin of the food will make it slightly more rubbery once dehydrated, and will lengthen the process of dehydration. Don't hesitate to try out different ways to determine which option you like best!

> **IMPORTANT NOTICE:** if your fruit and vegetables are not organic, prefer peeling them, since the peel might retain some pesticides, even after washing them.

Processing fruit and vegetables

Please note it is quite frequent for fruit and vegetables to take on a brown color while cooking, which does not always make them look good. If this detail bothers you, there are several solutions to keep their nice colour.

As mentioned earlier in this book, soaking the fruit for a few minutes in 3/4 water and 1/4 lemon juice will make them keep their color better, but also their taste and vitamins. It is especially good to dehydrate apricots, apples, pears or peaches.

For vegetables, the best way is to cook them quickly before dehydrating them. Carrots, eggplants or broccolis should be slightly steamed before they are dehydrated. Squash, potatoes, cauliflower can be blanched before they are dehydrated (meaning they are steamed or boiled for a few minutes, and then immersed in cold water). It is better to steam vegetables, since boiling water ruins vitamins and minerals.

Some vegetables, like mushrooms, garlic, onion or bell peppers, do not have to be blanched. It is not necessary either to pre-cook the herbs and plants you want to dehydrate.

If you are working with fruit that have a thick skin (like figs, plums or berries), it can be suggested to immerse them in boiling water for a couple of minutes before dehydration. This process will soften the skin and accelerate the dehydration process.

You could also consider using spices, honey, or sesame seeds to give more taste to your dehydrated fruit. But first, we suggest you try the process without this, to see if you enjoy your dried foods natural.

III. HOW TO USE A FOOD DEHYDRATOR

ARRANGE THE INGREDIENTS WELL

A dehydrator has several trays. Ideally, it is better to fill all the trays not to waste energy when using your dehydrator.

Save each tray for one type of fruit or vegetable. Since all ingredients don't have the same dehydrating time, this will enable you to take down the foods as they get dehydrated.

It is usually possible to dehydrate fruit and vegetables in the same batch, except for garlic and onion, which must be dehydrated separately (otherwise they make all other foods taste like garlic and onion!).

If you wish to dehydrate meat or fish, do it separately from fruit and vegetables, and thoroughly clean the trays after use.

> **IMPORTANT :** it is better never to interrupt the dehydration process while cooking. If you leave partially dehydrated food products on the trays in a dehydrator turned off, they might make mold very quickly. So avoid unplugging your device before all foods are ready.

HOW TO MAKE SURE THE FOODS ARE PROPERLY DEHYDRATED ?

If, with experience, you can dehydrate fruit and vegetables with your eyes closed, it is better to be twice as careful during your first attempts.

It is important to regularly monitor your dehydration trays, especially when you are dehydrating a food product for the very first time.

If a product is not dehydrated enough, it will still contain water and there's a risk it will quickly make mold. If the food is too dehydrated, it might lose its nutrients, be rubbery and taste less nice.

To know if a product is dehydrated enough, take it out of the device and leave it to cool for a couple of minutes. Regularly press the product and check it doesn't expel water. Cut it in half and check there is no humidity in the middle or on the edges.

Usually, a dehydrated piece of fruit looks like leather, and can be bent. A dehydrated vegetable in turn will be harder and crispier.

How to ideally store dehydrated foods ?

If you are not considering using your fruit and vegetables in the near future, once dehydrated they can be stored for a rather long time.

To store them well, arrange your foods in airtight jars, airtight boxes or vacuum packages, so they are not exposed to humidity and light. Humidity, in particular, is any dehydrated food's worst enemy (it makes them make mold in a couple of days).

Before storing your dehydrated food products in vacuum packages, leave them to cool. Otherwise, hot air might produce humidity in the vacuum box. Once the products are stored, shake the jars or bags over the following few days, and make sure there is no condensation (check for droplets under the lid). If the jars show some humidity, quickly put the foods in the dehydrator again, and store them back.

If you are interested in this topic, the last chapter of this book will come back in details on the preservation of dehydrated foods.

5. Dehydration time for the products

It must be noted that the dehydration time of a food product will always depend on the same criteria, namely the thickness of the slices, the ratio of water naturally present in the product, and the device power. The place and the time of year can also have an impact, since dehydrating will take less time if you live in a warm area.

For example, apricots take much longer to dry than bananas, since they contain a lot of water.

Dehydration time for a food product can also depend on your own tastes, whether you prefer your food crispy or a bit soft.

Please note that you should never add fresh foods during the dehydration process (i.e. if you already have foods that are partially dehydrated in your appliance). If you add a new tray while another one is already cooking, this might slow down the dehydration time of everything that is already in the appliance.

The following tables give you some information of the dehydration times to apply depending on the type of food products. But be careful: the indicated times may vary depending on the size of your slices or on the model you are using. When you are dehydrating a product for the first time, monitor the cooking process several times.

Dehydration time for fruit

Type of fruit	Dehydration time
Apricot	8 to 20 hours
Citrus fruit	4 to 12 hours
Cranberry	10 to 12 hours
Pineapple	10 to 18 hours
Banana	6 to 10 hours
Cherry	13 to 20 hours
Fig	8 to 20 hours

Strawberry	7 to 15 hours
Kiwi	7 to 15 hours
Melon	8 to 20 hours
Blueberry	8 to 18 hours
Nectarine	8 to 16 hours
Coconut	3 to 8 hours
Watermelon	8 to 10 hours
Peach	8 to 16 hours
Pear	8 to 16 hours
Apple	5 to 15 hours
Plum	20 to 28 hours
Grape	22 to 28 hours
Rhubarb	6 to 10 hours

DEHYDRATION TIME FOR VEGETABLES

TYPE OF VEGETABLES	DEHYDRATION TIME
Artichoke	6 to 12 hours
Asparagus	5 to 6 hours
Eggplant	4 to 8 hours
Beetroot	8 to 12 hours
Broccoli	10 to 14 hours
Carrot	6 to 10 hours
Celery	3 to 10 hours
Mushrooms	3 to 7 hours
Cabbage	7 to 11 hours
Cauliflower	6 to 14 hours
Pumpkin	7 to 11 hours
Cucumber	4 to 8 hours

III. HOW TO USE A FOOD DEHYDRATOR

Summer squash	10 to 14 hours
Winter squash	7 to 11 hours
Zucchini	7 to 11 hours
Bean	8 to 12 hours
Yam	7 to 11 hours
Corn	6 to 10 hours
Turnip	8 to 12 hours
Onion	4 to 8 hours
Parsnip	7 to 11 hours
Peas	4 to 8 hours
Bell pepper and hot pepper	4 to 8 hours
Potatoes	6 to 14 hours
Tomatoes	5 to 9 hours

OUR TIP: always remember to write down the exact dehydration time of your foods in a notebook. This way, you will be able to use your experience the next time you dehydrate the same type of fruit or vegetables.

6. DEHYDRATION TEMPERATURE OF THE PRODUCTS

6. DEHYDRATION TEMPERATURE OF THE PRODUCTS

As you have certainly guessed, the dehydration temperature of your foods is also quite a complex variable. All the more so since all food dehydrators do not necessarily allow you to regulate the cooking temperature.

The dehydration temperature of a food mainly depends on the type of food you wish to dehydrate.

As a general guideline, the following table gives you the recommended average temperature depending on the type of food you have to cook:

TYPE OF FOOD TO BE DEHYDRATED	RECOMMENDED TEMPERATURE	NOTES
Fruit and vegetables	Between 50 and 60°C / 122 and 140°F	A temperature set too high will prevent the preservation of some vitamins. A temperature set too low might not dehydrate the ingredient totally.
Meats	Over 70°C / 158°F	Opt for the highest possible temperature setting to prevent the spread of bacteria
Fish	Over 60°C / 140°F	As with meat, opt for the highest possible temperature setting.
Herbs, plants and spices	Between 30 and 40°C / 86 and 104°F	To keep the flavor of herbs and spices, cook them at a low temperature, for less than two hours.
Nuts and seeds	Between 30 and 40°C / 86 and 104°F	A temperature set too high might make the nuts rancid.
Yogurt	46°C / 114.8°F	It is imperative to be able to set your dehydrator on 46°C/ 114.8°F to make yoghurt in it.

As with the cooking time, dehydration temperature is no universal data.

Some would recommend for example that you do not go over 46°C/ 114.8°F, or even 43°C/ 109.4°F to dehydrate fruit and vegetables, to keep as much of their nutritional properties as possible. This choice will therefore depend on everyone's own preferences and experiences.

As far as meat and fish are concerned, it is nevertheless essential to use the highest possible temperature settings, to make sure bacteria are removed.

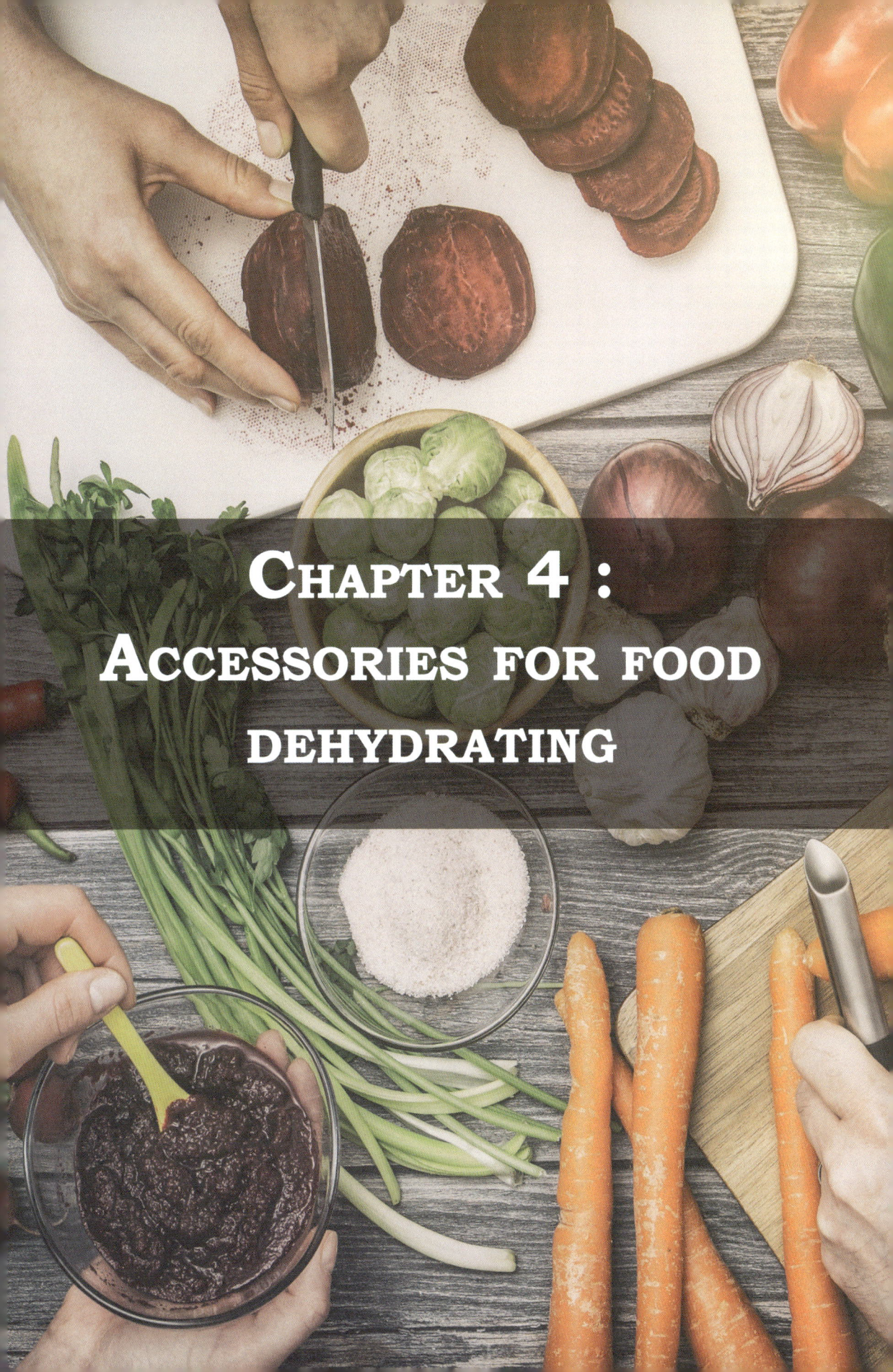

Chapter 4 : Accessories for food dehydrating

IV. Accessories for food dehydrating

Now that you are introduced to how to use your food dehydrator, it is time to have a look at the possible accessories that you will not be able to do without, or almost, to dehydrate your foods efficiently.

It is frequent that using a food dehydrator implies using various accessories or tools, that we are going to look at in detail in this chapter.

1. Accessories specific to your food dehydrator

First, you must know that some food dehydrator brands can sell model-specific accessories, or even spare parts.

The most common accessory is the extra tray or the replacement tray. If you have lost or damaged a tray, it is better indeed to buy a new one rather than to change the whole appliance!

If you buy a vertical airflow dehydrator, some brands sometimes sell extra trays, that would allow you to dehydrate more food products. Caution however: your food dehydrator might be less efficient if you buy too many trays.

For your information, a spare tray will cost between $12 and $50, depending on the brands. Likewise, you might sometimes find spare doors or lids on resale for your dehydrator. When contacting the manufacturer of your dehydrator, you might also be able to ask for a spare part (like a fan).

If you are looking for spare parts for your food dryer, the only solution might sometimes be to turn to the second-hand market.

In any case, always make sure to buy an accessory that is compatible with your dehydrator, so sold by the same brand and for the model you own.

> **IMPORTANT :** generally speaking, only upmarket food dehydrator brands will offer selling accessories or spare parts. There is indeed little interest in offering spare parts for a 50-dollar food dryer.

2. Useful accessories to prepare food

In parallel with the accessories directly linked to your food dryer, there are quite a few number of utensils or additional products that will prove very helpful when you will be preparing recipes in your dehydrator. Let's screen the kitchen equipment that is essential to successfully dehydrating foods.

Non-stick sheets

If, in most cases, food dehydration does not require the use of non-stick sheets, they can prove very handy for some recipes.

It must be noted that most recipes in the dehydrator might stick to the bottom of the appliance. It is the case for example if you are making fruit leather, crackers or recipes with caramel.

As soon as you are working with ingredients which are too liquid, or that might stick, it is necessary to invest in dehydrator non-stick sheets.

Favor non-stick sheets that are especially made for food dehydration, and reusable (they are usually made of food rated PTFE). On top of avoiding foods stuck at the bottom of the trays, this accessory will also facilitate cleaning your appliance.

Some food dehydration brands sell non-stick sheets specifically made for this or that model... but it is always possible to cut one of these sheets in two to adapt it to the dimensions of your trays.

Pricewise, you are looking at about $12 to buy a non-stick sheet, or even a package of three.

IV. ACCESSORIES FOR FOOD DEHYDRATING

THE PEELER

If mentioning this basic tool (that you probably already own!) could make you smile, it seems central to us to mention here how important the peeler is when processing dehydrated foods.

As seen in the previous chapter, most fruit and vegetables have to be peeled prior to dehydration. And this is where the peeler steps in!

As its name gives it away, the peeler allows you to peel fruit and vegetable with very little dent in the flesh (taking only the «peel»). Regarding food dehydration, which is itself going to make your foods shrink, keeping as much flesh as possible is crucial.

A peeler will cost around $1 to $12 on average. So it is clearly a very reasonable buy, and one which is going to be of great help!

> **OUR TIP:** it is better to invest in quality tools. True, a 1-dollar-peeler can be tempting in the shop, but it might give up the ghost after only a couple of uses

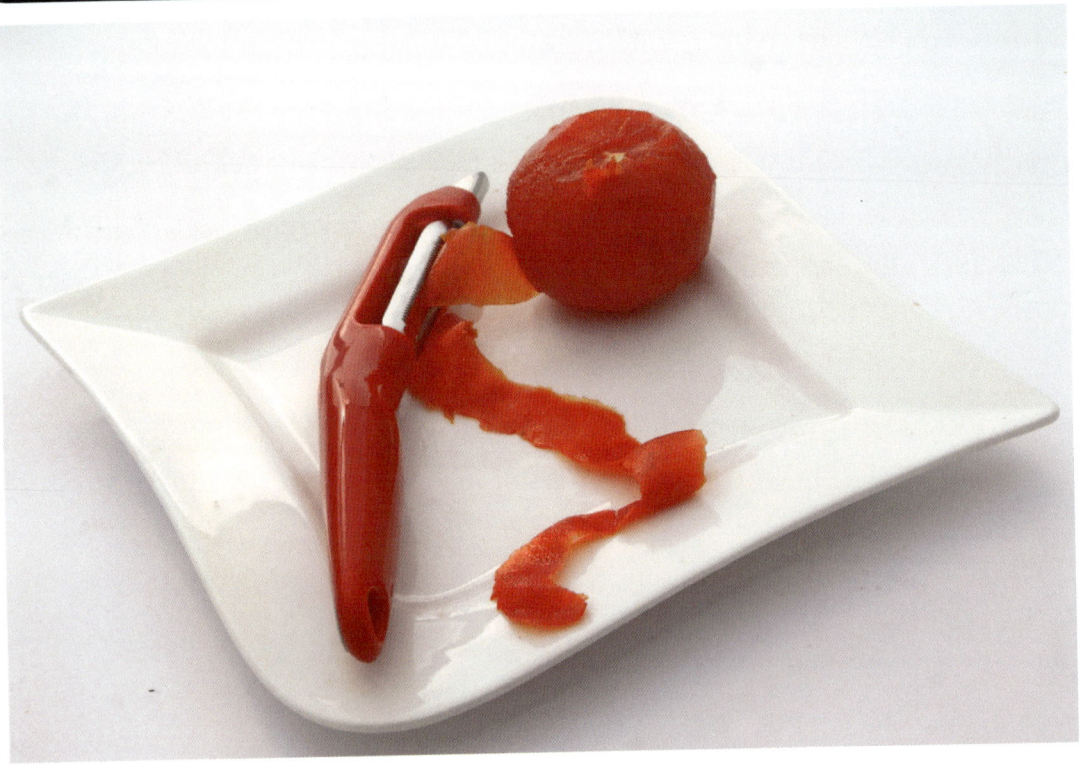

THE SLICER

Are your vegetables well peeled? You still have to slice them! If you are considering dehydrating a large quantity of foods, or making vegetables chips, buying a slicer (or mandoline) might prove essential. If the slicer is not necessarily crucial to anyone who has sharp knives, it is obvious that it allows for slicing the foods a lot faster, and a lot more even.

As mentioned, slicing your fruit and vegetables evenly is crucial to their dehydration. The slicer can help you along in this process and will be very practical if you work on large quantities of food.

Favor a slicer on which you can choose the thickness of the slices, because the necessary thickness will vary from one food to another. Depending on the models, a slicer can also help you cut the vegetables in different shapes.

Pricewise, you should count on $25 to $60 on average for a slicer. So this accessory will involve a bit of an investment, and we suggest you buy it only if you feel the use for it.

OUR TIP: since the slicer is a sharp and cutting utensil, we suggest you buy a model with a hand guard if you are not yet familiar with using one.

IV. ACCESSORIES FOR FOOD DEHYDRATING

The blender

Buying a blender is not essential to dehydrate foods, but you will see that it allows you to cook various recipes in the dehydrator.

For example, the blender proves very handy to prepare fruit leather or vegetable crackers. Some dehydrator recipes do involve mixing ingredients or preparing a batter.

You will also need it to grind dehydrated foods to powder. Ground dehydrated bananas or ground dehydrated oranges are perfect to bring out the taste of your desserts. You can also use ground dehydrated hot pepper or ground dried onions for your savoury dishes.

For food dehydration, you can either opt for a blender or for a food processor. Food processors are usually more expensive, but also more efficient than blenders to make fruit or vegetables purees.

A blender usually costs between $37 and $370 (count around $86 for a good-quality model). So you might want to wait and see whether you really need one for your recipes before you buy one.

2. USEFUL ACCESSORIES TO PREPARE FOOD

Preservation accessories

En dehors du matériel nécessaire à la préparation de vos aliments déshydratés, il peut être intéressant de réfléchir également à leur conservation.

Pour stocker vos aliments séchés, le plus élémentaire sera d'investir dans des bocaux hermétiques. Un bocal fermé permet de protéger vos aliments de l'humidité, et peut contenir une grande quantité d'aliments.

Si vous achetez un déshydrateur d'aliments dans l'optique de conserver vos aliments sur une très longue durée, nous vous conseillons également d'investir dans une emballeuse sous vide, qui va vous permettre de stocker vos aliments dans des sachets sous vide d'air.

Le dernier chapitre de cet ouvrage vous donne plus de conseils sur l'utilisation de ces deux accessoires.

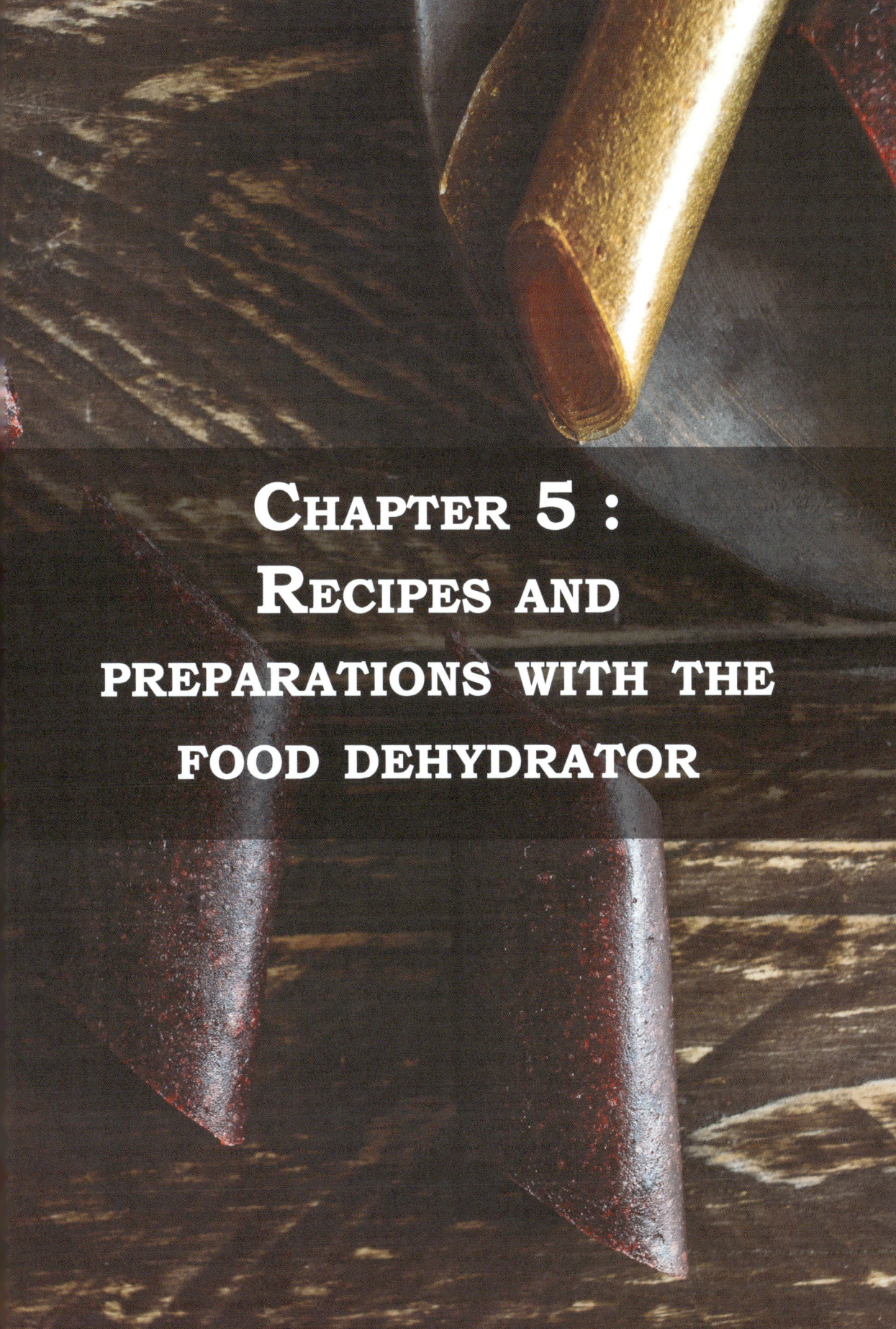

Chapter 5: Recipes and preparations with the food dehydrator

V. Recipes and preparations with the food dehydrator

You now know everything about the use of a food dryer, and you know about the essential equipment every owner of a food dehydrator should have. How about we move on to the next level?

We have told you about it earlier, the food dehydrator is not solely used to dehydrate food. Indeed, it can also be used to cook some unique and original recipes.

This chapter is going to give you lots of tips and hacks to cook whatever crosses your mind thanks to your appliance.

1. Fruit leather

1. Fruit Leather

Fruit leather is made with one or several mashed fruits, just like fruit puree, and then dried in the dehydrator to harden it. The texture and taste of fruit leather make it the perfect snack for those who don't fancy fresh fruit, and this recipe also allows you to preserve your fruit better!

Fruit leather can be cooked with any type of fruits, just as long as the fruit puree is not too liquid. You can also add spices, honey or sweetening elements (dates, sugar, etc) to it.

Fruit leather recipe

To make fruit leather, you will need:

- Fresh fruits,
- A sharp knife to prepare them,
- A blender to mix them,
- A spatula,
- Non-stick sheets for the dehydrator,
- And of course your dehydrator.

Once you have everything you need, you can make your own fruit leather. The technique is quick and easy:

1. Wash your fruit, peel them, remove the seeds and stalks, and slice or chop them finely.
2. Mix the fruit bits in your blender to get a thick fruit puree. If the mix is too thick, you can add a little water. In place of a blender, you can also stew the fruits.
3. Pour the resulting fruit puree on a dehydrator non-stick sheet.
4. Using a spatula, flatten the mix until it is about 0.5cm / 0.2in thick.
5. You can add seeds, nuts or coconut flakes on top of your fruit leather before cooking it (optional). If you do that, you will have to store your fruit leather in the fridge afterwards.
6. Lay the non-stick sheet to dry in the dehydrator, between 46°C/ 114.8°F and 54°C/ 129°F for at least 5 hours.

V. RECIPES AND PREPARATIONS WITH THE FOOD DEHYDRATOR

7. To know whether your leather is cooked through, don't open your dehydrator before the required 5 hours. With a knife, pull the corners of the batter and pierce a hole in the middle of the leather: if your mix is still sticky, it means the process is not finished yet.

8. Once the leather is cooked through, you can roll it and cut it in pieces of the length of your choice. Slice it before it cools down, or it will be harder to cut.

You can then store your fruit slices in an airtight container, and eat them up whenever you feel like it! If you are not planning on using or savoring your fruit leather soon, you can preserve them for two months in an airtight container. Beyond that period, you should preserve them in the fridge or in the freezer.

> **OUR TIP:** to make sure your fruit leather is completely dehydrated, set the timer of your dehydrator on 10 hours. To speed up the dehydration process, you can also take the juice of the fruit stew away. It is also interesting to add a banana if your fruit contain too much humidity, to get a puree that will get dehydrated faster.

HOW TO USE FRUIT LEATHER ?

Fruit leather can of course be eaten as it is, and replace any sweet or candy. We would then suggest eating it in reasonable quantities and avoid adding sugar to the mix (fruit already naturally contain sugar).

Note that one of the advantages of fruit leather is that it allows you to prepare fruit which are slightly more damaged than dehydrated fruit. If you fruit seem a bit too ripe to be dehydrated as they are, blend them and make fruit leather with them!

Fruit leather can accompany various recipes such as homemade cakes... or be used as a mix with your yoghurts.

Fruit leather cake

If you were used to using dried fruit or fruit chips to fill your cakes, here is an original recipe to get the best out of fruit leather:

- Pick up 2 pieces of fruit, one sweet and one sour; take for example banana and grapefruit.

- Make two separate fruit leathers with them, and while they are dehydrating, get started with the cake mix.

Once everything is ready, alternate one layer of cake, one layer of cream and finally one layer of fruit leather. Sure success !

Fruit leather cereals

Fruit leather is ideal for those who enjoy cereals for breakfast. Here is how to use them:

- Buy plain cereals. Favor oat flakes or muesli (these are better, since they contain less fat and less sugar than the others).
- In your bowl, incorporate fruit leather pieces before adding milk or yoghurt.

If necessary, add a little honey or sugar (but it is far from essential!).

2. MUESLI

Store-bought cereals are often loaded with sugar... unlike homemade muesli! Preparing your own muesli recipe will give you control over what you or your children eat for the most important meal of the day.

The good news? Your food dryer allows you to prepare your own muesli. All you need is the right recipe.

MUESLI RECIPE

If you wish to make your own muesli in the dehydrator, you will need to gather the following elements:

- 1 1/2 cups of plain oat flakes,
- 1/2 cup of sunflower seeds,
- 1/4 cup of sesame seeds,
- 1/2 cup of coconut flakes with no added sugar,
- 1/4 cup of buckwheat groats,
- 2 teaspoons of ground cinnamon,
- A pinch of salt,
- 1/4 cup of maple syrup,
- 1 tablespoon of coconut oil,
- A sachet a vanilla sugar,
- 1 dehydrator non-stick sheet,
- And of course your food dehydrator.

Once you have all these elements, here is how to make your homemade muesli:

1. In a bowl, mix all the dry ingredients (sunflower seeds, sesame seeds, oat flakes, coconut, buckwheat).

2. Add your muesli seasoning (maple syrup, coconut oil, salt, vanilla sugar) and mix.

3. Pour everything on the non-stick sheet, in the dehydrator, and set to dehydrate for 5 hours at about 45°C/ 113°F.

4. Once the muesli is ready, leave to cool. Then place it in a closed jar, to be kept in your cellar or in the fridge.

You can adjust the cooking time to your preference regarding crunchiness. You can also vary the seeds or ingredients in the recipe. Why not adding a few nuts?

Choose for example pistachios, cashew or pecan nuts. Favor of course «plain» and unsalted nuts.

HOW TO ENJOY YOUR MUESLI ?

Muesli is ideal to start the day right, or as a snack. Mix it ideally in a small bowl, to limit the intake.

Don't hesitate to add fruit, dehydrated or fresh, to complement your cereals.

If you think your muesli is a bit bland, you can add a sweetening product. Options are plenty, but whatever your choice may be, be reasonable. The following ingredients can add the extra taste you are after:

- Molasses,
- Honey,
- Brown sugar,
- Cinnamon,
- Toasted coconut,
- Lemon juice,
- Agave syrup,
- Maple syrup,
- Nut butter.

Feel also free to add milk, non-dairy milk or yoghurt to avoid getting cereals which are too dry.

3. Vegetable bouillon powder

The food dryer is ideal if you want to prepare homemade vegetable bouillon powder, which you can use to season your dishes, soups or broths.

The point of making your own vegetable bouillon powder with a dehydrator is that you will get a healthy and natural bouillon powder, without too much salt and preservatives (unlike those you can buy in shops, which are usually loaded with salt).

To prepare delicious dehydrated vegetable bouillon powders, you will just have to dry your vegetables and herbs in the dehydrator before mixing them with a blender.

V. RECIPES AND PREPARATIONS WITH THE FOOD DEHYDRATOR

THE RECIPE FOR VEGETABLE BOUILLON POWDER

To prepare your own bouillon powder at home, you just have to gather the following elements:

- 2 carrots,
- 2 celery stalks,
- 1 potato
- 2 tomatoes,
- 4 button mushrooms,
- 2 cabbage leaves,
- 1 handful of parsley,
- 2 garlic cloves,
- Salt, pepper, dill powder, turmeric powder, nutmeg,
- a blender
- And your food dehydrator.

Once you have all the ingredients, you can get started:

1. Start by cleaning, peeling and finely slicing the vegetables with a slicer.

2. On your dehydrator trays, arrange the vegetables (carrots, celery, potato, tomatoes, mushroom, cabbage leaf, parsley, garlic) and dehydrate for about 7 hours at 50°C/ 122°F.

3. Make sure the vegetables are fully dehydrated, and leave them to cool down for about twenty minutes.

4. Put all the dehydrated vegetables and the seasoning (salt, pepper, dill powder, turmeric powder, nutmeg) in the blender bowl and mix until you get a fine powder.

Your vegetable bouillon powder is ready! You just have to preserve it in an airtight container (such as a glass jar) and keep it handy in your kitchen.

TIP: remember to label your jars if you are making several bouillon powders, so that you find the right one and adapt your recipes every time of the year. This recipe is a good way to use surplus vegetables and avoid food waste while seasoning your dishes!

How to use vegetable bouillon powder ?

Your vegetable bouillon powder is simply a great seasoning to prepare your courses. It enhances their taste and is 100% healthy and vegetarian.

Vegetable bouillon powder can be used in cooking water for rice, bulgur, lentils and pasta, to slightly give these various ingredients taste. It is also possible to sprinkle your bouillon powder directly onto your pan, for example to season a vegetable stir-fry or any other course.

You can also use it straight to make… broth! It will then flavor your water and give your broth a much better taste.

As you will notice if you become an enthusiast of this magic powder, it can be used it almost any savory dish! This bouillon powder is actually a perfect alternative to salt.

V. RECIPES AND PREPARATIONS WITH THE FOOD DEHYDRATOR

4. Vegetable chips

If you have children that are not too keen on eating fresh vegetables, you could try and bribe them with vegetable chips! Vegetable chips are nothing else but dehydrated and seasoned vegetables, which are delicious as snacks or before the meal.

Although it must be confessed that vegetable chips should not be eaten in excess, they remain a healthier alternative to chips and other snacks available in shops.

Vegetable chips recipe

To prepare vegetable chips, you will need the following:

- Vegetables (zucchini, potatoes, beetroots, turnips…),
- 1 tablespoon of olive oil,
- Salt,
- Parsley,
- 1 garlic clove,
- A slicer,
- A dehydrator.

Once you have all this at your fingertips, here are the various steps for the recipe:

1. Start by cleaning the vegetables, and peeling them if necessary.

2. With a slicer, slice the vegetables in fine slices of about 2mm/ 0.08in. Slices must be as thin as possible.

3. You can boil the slices for a couple of minutes in a pot of boiling water, to help them retain their nice color. Immerse them in cold water right after boiling.

4. Arrange the vegetable slices on a platter. Sprinkle with a pinch of salt and some olive oil. Mix and leave on the side for 15 minutes.

5. Pour the liquid out of the dish, and add some chopped parsley and the garlic clove you will have previously crunched and chopped to your vegetables. Mix it all.

6. Arrange the slices of seasoned vegetables on the dehydrator trays. Make sure they are not in contact with each other. Set on about 45°C/ 113°F.

7. Vegetable chips cook for about 5 to 25 hours on average, depending on the type of vegetables.

It is important to keep an eye on the cooking process, as always with food dehydration. If you think it is dehydrated enough, take out a few chips, leave them to cool down for about an hour and make sure the chips are crispy.

How to enjoy vegetable chips ?

As you can well imagine, vegetable chips make perfect snacks before the meal. They usually look nicer and are less salty than shop-bought chips.

Caution though, this does not mean they are healthy for you! As for any snacks, vegetable chips are easy to nibble on, and it is not long before you eat too many of them if you're not watching yourself… You've been warned!

To make an even nicer arrangement, do combine several kinds of vegetables, so that you have multi-colored chips. It is also an option to try and cut the veggies in sticks, to shape them like fries.

V. RECIPES AND PREPARATIONS WITH THE FOOD DEHYDRATOR

Please note that you can store your veggie chips for more than one year, if they are kept in a jar, away from light and humidity.

> **OUR TIP:** Go ahead and try different herbs and seasonings for your chips, until you find «your» ideal recipe for veggie chips.

5. MAKING YOGHURT WITH THE DEHYDRATOR

In case you didn't know, the food dehydrator works exactly like a yoghurt maker. It is therefore possible, in theory, to make homemade yoghurts with it.

To do so, there are two requirements:

- Your dehydrator offers a setting option at 46°C/ 114.8°F,
- And it must be high enough to accommodate yoghurt glass containers.

Some food dehydrators are sold with special compartments to make yoghurt. If you have a horizontal airflow dehydrator, you usually just need to take all the trays away to fit your yoghurt pots in it.

To make yoghurt in your dehydrator, you will need the following ingredients:

- 1 litre/ 0.26 US gal lqd of milk
- 1 plain yoghurt,
- 2 tablespoons of milk powder,
- Glass containers,
- A food dehydrator.

To make your own yoghurt, just follow these steps:

1. In a bowl, mix together the milk, the yoghurt and the milk powder. Stir to avoid clumps. We need a shop-bought yoghurt because it contains the lactic ferments which are essential to the process.
2. Pour the (liquid) mix in the glass containers.

3. Put the containers in the pre-heated dehydrator (46°C/ 114.8°F) without their lids.

4. Wait for about 6 to 12 hours. The longer the wait, the creamier the yoghurts.

Once they are ready, leave them to cool in the fridge. You can then enjoy them with some sugar, honey, and why not some dehydrated fruit!

CAUTION: homemade yoghurts do not contain any preservatives. If it is healthier, this also means you can only keep them for a couple of days…

6. Dried meat

If food dehydration is very appreciated by vegetarians, it must not be forgotten that a dehydrator also allows you to prepare delicious dried meat recipes.

It must be noted though that preparing dried meat in a dehydrator requires a bit of skill, and a good-quality appliance.

Moreover, you will have to pay special attention to the quality of the meat, which must be very fresh when being dehydrated.

The recipe for Beef Jerky

Let's see together how to make Beef Jerky, namely slices of seasoned and dried beef, of which Americans are great fans.

To make Beef Jerky, you will need the following:

- Beef meat (that you are going to slice),
- 1/4 cup soy sauce,
- 2 tablespoons of Worcestershire sauce,
- 1/2 teaspoon of red pepper,
- 1 teaspoon of pepper,

6. DRIED MEAT

- 1 teaspoon of paprika,
- 1 teaspoon of garlic powder,
- 1 teaspoon of onion powder,
- Salt,
- Dehydrator non-stick sheets,
- And of course your food dehydrator.

Opt for meat that has as little fat as possible, since fat does not do well with dehydration. Once you have all the ingredients, here is how to prepare your own Beef Jerky:

1. Start by mixing all the ingredients (except the meat) to make a thick sauce, which you are going to use as a marinade. In the mix, apply a ratio of one teaspoon of salt per kilo (/per 2.2 lb) (the salt does not so much enhance the taste but rather avoids bacteria spread).

2. It is a good idea to refrigerate the meat for 30 minutes before processing it, to slice it more easily.

3. Cut the meat lengthwise, then in its thickness, to make thin strips. It is better to have thin slices, otherwise the dehydration process would be long and tedious. Cut and remove the fat, which must not be dehydrated. Next, arrange the meat on a large dish.

4. Put the meat in a bowl and cover it with the sauce. Stir to permeate the meat with the sauce. Leave to marinate for about 10 hours in the fridge.

5. It is now time to dehydrate it at a minimum temperature of 70°C/ 158°F (ideally, use the highest possible temperature setting on your device). Use a non-stick sheet and arrange the strips next to each other. This process usually takes from four to seven hours. However, you should always check on your meat after the first 90 minutes.

Once the meat is totally dry, cover it with kitchen paper and leave it to cool. The kitchen paper is going to absorb the excess fat. Then put it in resealable bags, in a dry place.

Once the meat is totally dry, cover it with kitchen paper and leave it to cool. The kitchen paper is going to absorb the excess fat. Then put it in resealable bags, in a dry place.

It is possible to dry other meats than beef, though you should favor lean meat which keeps for longer. Thus, you can use pork (tenderloin), turkey, chicken, duck (breast), horsemeat or game. Bones and fat must be systematically removed.

Of course, only use meat which is fresh and free of all threat of bacteria spread. To be on the safe side, you can pre-cook the meat before preparing it, then heat up your Jerky right after processing it for about 30 minutes in an oven pre-heated at 70 °C/158°F.

If you are using game, you should freeze the meat for at least 60 days before preparing your Jerky, to make sure there are no germs and bacteria in it.

Please note it is important not to dehydrate meat together with other ingredients (fruit and vegetables), since the meat would flavor your other foods.

> **CAUTION:** all food dehydrators do not allow you to dehydrate meat. Some appliances are designed exclusively for fruit and vegetables. So be careful to choose an equipment that is designed also to dry meat (i.e. which can heat up to 70 °C/ 158°C and higher). When you are preparing meat or fish, always set your device on the highest possible temperature.

How to enjoy Beef Jerky ?

Just like veggie chips, Beef Jerky is first and foremost a snack, enough in itself. So you can store your strips away from light and in a dry place, and enjoy them every now and then.

Beef Jerky is rich in proteins, so it is something useful to take with you for a hike or a picnic. You can also consider rehydrating it, for example by adding it to some ramen (Japanese noodle broth) or soup.

Once again, be careful not to over-indulge in this snack, which is of course a bit rich!

Please note that drying your food remains an excellent way to preserve your meat. It is judged that you can keep Beef Jerky for a year if it is stored in a vacuum bag, and even longer if it is frozen. At room temperature, it can be kept for about three to four weeks.

7. Dried fish

Fish lovers may be reassured: a dehydrator also allows you to dehydrate fish, to make delicious «Fish Jerky».

Fish like salmon, tuna, mackerel, cod or sardines are perfect for dehydration. Once more, you will have to pay special attention to the freshness of the fish before you dehydrate it.

The recipe for Fish Jerky

If you wish to make a delicious snack with dry fish, you are going to need the following:

- Fish,
- Coarse salt,
- Pepper,
- Two tablespoons of soy sauce,
- Dehydrator non-stick sheets,
- And your food dehydrator.

Once you have all this, here is how to prepare your Fish Jerky:

1. Start by removing the guts of the fish to keep only the flesh.

2. Clean the fish and refrigerate it for half an hour before you cut it.

3. Cut the fish in thin, even slices.

4. Place the fish in a bowl full of salted water. Use three tablespoons of coarse salt. Leave on the side for 30 minutes, then rinse and clean the fish with a clean kitchen towel.

5. Next, arrange the fish on a flat dish and cover it with coarse salt. You usually need one tablespoon of salt per kilo/2.2 lb of fish. Add the pepper, the soy sauce, mix and refrigerate for about 6 to 8 hours.

6. Arrange the fish slices in the dehydrator, on non-stick sheets. Do not hesitate to remove any excess coarse salt. Set the dehydrator at a minimum temperature of 60°C/ 140°F (ideally, use the highest temperature setting on your appliance), for about 8 to 12 hours.

Don't hesitate to regularly check on the fish. It should be firm and dry, but should not crumble.

Once the fish is ready, leave it to cool, and store it in vacuum bags or glass jars, away from light in a dry place.

As for meat, do not dehydrate fish together with other ingredients (fruit and vegetables), since your fish might transfer its taste to the rest of the «batch».

How to enjoy Fish Jerky ?

Fish Jerky is first and foremost a snack, just like Beef Jerky. You can have it before the meal, or when travelling.

If you like fish, you can vary using various fish and other marinades. You can use for example Teriyaki sauce (Japanese sauce).

You can take Fish Jerky anywhere with you. Rich in salt and proteins, it is perfect as a snack for sportspeople who love casting off for adventure.

Careful, dried fish cannot be kept as long as dried beef. Fat fish (like salmon) can be kept for a much shorter time than lean fish (like sole). It is better to eat it within two weeks at the longest. Failing that, you can keep it in the fridge.

8. Tomato sauce

Since we are talking about savory ingredients, it seems to the point to mention dehydrated veggies! If you have had enough of buying tomato sauce at the grocery store, but don't have time to cook your own tomato sauce on a regular basis, your dehydrator could very well help you out here…

Indeed, food dehydration can allow you to create a universal mix for your tomato sauce, tomato concentrate and tomato soups.

The recipe for tomato sauce with the dehydrator

To make your own tomato sauce, all you have to do is gather the following:

- 6 to 8 kg of ripe tomatoes (13.3 to 17.6 lb)
- 4 green peppers
- 3 onions
- 3 carrots,
- 1 garlic clove,
- Dehydrator non-stick sheets,
- A colander,
- A blender
- A food dehydrator.

Once you have all this, here is how to proceed:

1. Clean the tomatoes and the peppers, and chop them small.
2. Peel the onions, the garlic and the carrots, and chop them small.
3. Blend all the ingredients, until you have a thick paste.
4. Sieve the mix to remove the tomato pulp.
5. Cook the mix in a large pot without the lid, on medium heat for 5 hours. Stir from time to time to prevent the mix from sticking to the pot.
6. Once the paste is nice and thick (ideally, it should stick to the spoon), spread it on the non-stick sheets.

7. Put the sheets in the dehydrator on 60°C/ 140°F, until the paste is perfectly crunchy.

8. Once the mix is ready, blend it to get a powder.

You can store this powder in glass jars, to use it year-round.

How to use my tomato sauce ?

Your dehydrated tomato sauce will just need to be rehydrated so you can use it whenever you need it. You just have to add water to get a sauce or a hearty paste.

Use a teaspoonful of water for one teaspoonful of powder to get tomato concentrate. Use three teaspoonfuls of water for one teaspoonful of powder to get tomato sauce.

By adding more water, you can enjoy a delicious tomato juice. Your powder mix can also be used in soups, or to season your sauces.

9. Unusual uses of a food dehydrator

As you get it, if the usual scope of food dehydration is wide, you should know that the only limitation to it is your imagination. Indeed, you will discover as you use it that your food dehydrator can be used in many different ways.

Here are a few «misuses» of your food dehydrator that might inspire you further:

- You can give a renewed crunchiness to your food that has softened because of humidity, for example cereal bars that have stayed in the cupboard for a bit too long... A few minutes in the dehydrator, and here we go!

- Making breadcrumbs become easy as pie. If you have some leftover bread, dehydrate it together with herbs for more flavor and blend it all. Now you can enjoy homemade nuggets, breaded fish and escalope!

- If you are a homemade bread or pizza enthusiast, you can also raise dough in the dehydrator or dry your fresh pasta in it to accelerate the process.

- Make your own fire-starters. You just need to get citrus fruit peels (which do not decay because of their antibacterial properties), slice them and dehydrate them. The oils they contain are flammable and will allow you to start the fireplace without any chemicals.

- You can also prepare your own herbal teas by dehydrating plants, herbs, flowers... following your taste and their properties. You will, at the same time, perfume your home with their scents. Thyme has anti-infective and antiseptic properties, so it can clean-up the air you breathe, and it can avoid and cure ENT and bronchopulmonary infections when used as herbal tea.

- Dehydrating spices and aromatics is a good way to preserve them. Dehydrated aromatics will have a bit less flavor than fresh ones, but will be more concentrate. It will also, and that's a very good point, be available year-round!

- Dehydrating plants, flowers, citrus fruit peels and spices will allow you to make original and varied potpourris or just an herbarium if you are a lover of plants and how to use them, or for your children with an educational purpose for example.

Always remember to adjust the temperature of your dehydrator for each recipe. To make potpourri and dehydrate plants and aromatics, never heat over 40°C/ 104°F.

Chapter 6: Storing and using dehydrated foods

VI. Storing and using dehydrated foods

You are now an expert in the art of food dehydration. But if there is something that must not be neglected, it is how to store your dehydrated foods. Although we have already briefly mentioned storage in the previous chapters, it seems useful to sum up here everything there is to know on this topic.

Indeed, dehydrating foods is an efficient way to preserve them for longer. But to avoid having to throw away your dehydrated foods, you have to do everything to store them the best possible way!

1. STORING DEHYDRATED FOODS: GOOD PRACTICES

We have already been over it, food dehydration kills bacteria, and so allows for a much longer storage of food. Dehydrated fruit and vegetables can often be kept for a year, or even longer.

The other side of the coin? Dehydrated foods become extremely sensitive to humidity and bacteria. If they are not stored properly, they might make mold. And it would be a shame to waste food you have taken hours to carefully prepare.

You should know there are different ways to store dehydrated foods. For each method, it is important to wait until the foods have cooled down before storing them. We also advise you to wash your hands thoroughly, or even to wear gloves, if you are touching the foods when you are storing them.

Store them as soon as they are cooled down. Indeed, waiting too long to store your dehydrated foods increases the risk they get contaminated by ambient humidity or insects. Foods like dried tomatoes or dehydrated onions are very sensitive to ambient humidity.

Regardless of the type of container you choose to store your foods in, always label them. Write down the type of food (if necessary, i.e. if stored in a non-see-through container), date of dehydration and why not the weight. Writing down the date is essential, since it will allow you to use your dehydrated foods in the order they have been prepared.

Ideally, store your foods in a dry and dark place (the cellar or the garage usually remain the best choices).

2. Preserving in jars

Here is a tip if you decide to go for preserving dehydrated foods: start making room for glass jars!

A glass jar is ideal to store dehydrated foods, since it protect them perfectly from humidity. It will have of course to be perfectly air-tight, so closed with a lid (usually metallic).

Glass being see-through, you can easily find this or that dehydrated food. On the downside, it lets the light go through. So store your jars in the cellar, or in a cupboard (well away from any source of light).

You can also go for iron jars, that stop all light. But it is imperative that the jar should be air-tight (and therefore closed with a lid, usually made of plastic).

Over the first days, remember to shake the jars regularly, and make sure there is no condensation inside. If there is, you might have to repeat the dehydration process, because this means your foods still contain moisture.

You can find storing jars in the shops, but the most budget-friendly option is to buy food canned in jars (vegetables, fruit puree, jam, etc.) and keep the jars when they are empty.

It is better not to store different foods in the same jar, so there is no flavor transfer.

VI. STORING AND USING DEHYDRATED FOODS

HOW TO STERILIZE JARS ?

Unlike fruit preserves, sterilizing glass jars is not necessary to preserve dehydrated foods. But if you want to make sure you have perfectly sterilized jars, here is how:

1. Boil water in a pot.

2. Immerse the jars in the boiling water.

3. Leave the jars in the water for 10 minutes starting at boiling point.

4. Let the jars dry bottom up on a clean tea towel.

3. VACUUM PACKING

If preserving in jars is the easiest way, it is not the most perfect one! Indeed, foods preserved in jars might lose their taste and their colors.

If you are planning on storing your dehydrated foods for more than 6 months, it might be better to opt for another preservation method: vacuum packing.

3. VACUUM PACKING

Vacuum packing is the best preservation technique to keep both the color and the flavor of your foods in the long term.

It consists in arranging your dehydrated foods in plastic bags, and suck the air out thanks to a vacuum-sealer. This way your foods will remain edible after one year.

For this type of preservation, you just have to let your foods cool down, and then place them in a plastic bag. The vacuum-sealer is going to suck the air out of the bag, and seal it. Next, store away from light, for example in a metallic or plastic box.

Pack one type of food at a time, to avoid flavor or moisture transfer.

Regarding the bags, opt for plastic freezer bags, since all bags are not necessarily air-tight and therefore not suitable for vacuum packing.

Also note that there are vacuum-packers that vacuum jars, thus joining the advantages of jars and of vacuum-packing. Caution, you must use jars designed to this use, that will not break during the process!

VI. STORING AND USING DEHYDRATED FOODS

4. FREEZING DEHYDRATED FOOD

Should you ever ask yourself, do know it is absolutely possible to freeze dehydrated foods. You have to place them in freezer bags, or specific containers.

You can keep you dehydrated foods even longer thanks to freezing. But please note that they might lose their nutritional value. So freezing is only interesting for a long term storage, or if you don't have the time or the equipment to store your foods in another way.

Various cautions must be taken if you want to freeze your foods:

- Only freeze small quantities at a time.
- Write down the date of freezing on the packages.
- Only freeze fresh food once, never refreeze thawed dishes.

The freezing process is going to be different depending on the type of food. Dehydrated fruit and vegetables can be cooked frozen without any problem, but it is better to let them thaw at room temperature.

This is different from meat products, which must thaw in the fridge and not on the countertop.

Note that it is possible to rehydrate your foods while thawing. The rehydration process is explained in the next chapter.

In any case, dehydrating food that is to freeze can prove practical if you are processing a large quantity of food, and that you need to optimize your storage space.

5. Rehydrating foods

If it is important to know how to store dehydrated foods, it is also useful to know how to rehydrate them if needed!

Indeed, if you use food dehydration to preserve your fruit and vegetables, you will surely be interested in rehydrating them. Good news, rehydrating food is far from difficult.

To rehydrate foods, you just have to soak them in a bowl of water. Foods must be fully immersed over a period lasting from 30 minutes to 2 hours. It is better to use boiling water, which noticeably shortens the time necessary to rehydration. Note it is perfectly possible to soak frozen dehydrated foods to rehydrate them.

For fruit, it is an option to soak them in vegetable or fruit juice to rehydrate them. In that case, put the bowl with the soaking fruit in the fridge to avoid any contamination.

If you are directly cooking dehydrated foods, remember to add their equivalent in water to the pot, to prevent them from soaking up the juices.

Keep in mind that a rehydrated food will not be exactly the same as a fresh food, since it will rehydrate to a maximum of 80%.

If it is possible to rehydrate dry meat, we advise you NOT to rehydrate dry fish, because it will taste bad!

As always regarding dehydration, and cooking in general, we invite you to try out your own procedures and recipes, to know which foods you'd rather rehydrate or eat dehydrated.

Conclusion

Thank you for reading our guide on food dehydration through and through. Now, you can brag about your perfect knowledge of food dehydration.

The many recipes and mixes with delicious dried fruit and vegetables, Beef Jerky and other delicacies from the food dehydrator are all yours!

As you will soon become aware of if you are new to the art of dehydration, it is first and foremost a question of experience. You might in the upcoming weeks cook some delicious recipes... and others not so delicious!

The most important is never to stop experimenting, and always take the time to write down your discoveries. Try with different temperatures, cooking times, ingredients to dehydrate, herbs and spices you use in your mixes, the way you cut the ingredients, processing (or not) the ingredients prior to dehydrating them...

All the solutions are here for you to try, and it is only by using your device on a regular basis that you will end up deciding on the type of dehydrated foods your like best, and that you will learn how to get your recipes right every time.

It is only with try-outs that you are going to master your food dehydrator to perfection, and make it one of your favourite household appliances. Enjoy your recipes!

Appendix: The Seasonality Table

If you are looking for cheap fruit and vegetables, and ideally, at your local producer's, it is important to know about the seasonality of fruit and vegetables.

This seasonality table will guide you year-round, and will help you choose the foods you should buy in priority depending on the time of the year:

January

Fruits	Vegetables	
Lemon	Garlic	Onion
Kiwi	Beetroot	Leek
Tangerine	Carrot	Potatoes
Orange	Celery	Spinach
Grapefruit	Brussels sprout	Turnip
Pear	Squash	
Apple	Endive	

February

Fruits	Vegetables	
Lemon	Garlic	Leek
Kiwi	Beetroot	Potatoes
Tangerine	Carrot	Lamb's lettuce
Orange	Celery	Turnip
Grapefruit	Brussels sprout	Onion
Pear	Endive	
Apple	Frisée salad	

March

Fruits	Vegetables	
Lemon	Asparagus	Leek
Kiwi	Beetroot	Potatoes
Orange	Chard	Spinach
Grapefruit	Carrot	Frisée salad
Pear	Celery	Turnip
Apple	Brussels sprout	Onion
	Endive	

April

Fruits	Vegetables	
Lemon	Asparagus	Leek
Grapefruit	Beetroot	Potatoes
Apple	Chard	Radish
Rhubarb	Carrot	Turnip
	Endive	Onion
	Spinach	

May

Fruits	Vegetables	
Cherry	Garlic	Zucchini
Strawberry	Asparagus	Spinach
Raspberry	Eggplant	Lettuce
Rhubarb	Beetroot	Turnip
	Chard	Onion
	Carrot	Pea
	Celery	Leek
	Cauliflower	Potatoes
	Cucumber	Radish

JUNE

Fruits	Vegetables	
Apricot	Garlic	Zucchini
Blackcurrant	Artichoke	Spinach
Cherry	Eggplant	Fennel
Strawberry	Beetroot	Lettuce
Raspberry	Chard	Turnip
Redcurrant	Carrot	Onion
Melon	Celery	Pea
Apple	White cabbage	Bell pepper
	Cauliflower	Potatoes
	Cucumber	Radish

JULY

Fruits	Vegetables	
Apricot	Garlic	Fennel
Blackcurrant	Artichoke	Bean
Cherry	Asparagus	Lettuce
Fig	Eggplant	Corn
Strawberry	Beetroot	Onion
Rapsberry	Chard	Leek
Redcurrant	Carrot	Pea
Melon	Celery	Bell pepper
Mirabelle	White cabbage	Potatoes
Nectarine	Cauliflower	Radish
Peach	Cucumber	Tomatoes
Apple	Zucchini	
Plum	Spinach	

AUGUST

Fruits	Vegetables	
Apricot	Garlic	Bean
Blackcurrant	Artichoke	Lettuce
Fig	Eggplant	Corn
Melon	Beetroot	Onion
Blackberry	Chard	Leek
Redcurrant	Carrot	Bell pepper
Nectarine	Celery	Potatoes
Watermelon	White cabbage	Radish
Peach	Cauliflower	Tomatoes
Pear	Cucumber	
Apple	Zucchini	
Plum	Spinach	
Prune	Fennel	

SEPTEMBER

Fruits	Vegetables	
Melon	Garlic	Cucumber
Blackberry	Artichoke	Zucchini
Blueberry	Eggplant	Spinach
Grapefruit	Beetroot	
Watermelon	Chard	
Peach	Broccoli	
Pear	Carrot	
Apple	Celery	
Prune	White cabbage	
Plum	Cauliflower	
Grape	Brussels sprout	

October

Fruits	Vegetables	
Quince	Garlic	Endive
Grapefruit	Eggplant	Spinach
Pear	Beetroot	Fennel
Apple	Broccoli	Frisée salad
Grape	Carrot	Bean
	Celery	Lettuce
	White cabbage	Lamb's lettuce
	Cauliflower	Corn
	Brussels sprout	Onion
	Cucumber	Leek
	Squash	Potatoes
	Zucchini	Radish

November

Fruits	Vegetables	
Quince	Garlic	Fennel
Tangerine	Beetroot	Frisée salad
Kiwi	Broccoli	Lettuce
Orange	Carrot	Lamb's lettuce
Grappefruit	Celery	Spinach
Pear	White cabbage	Turnip
Apple	Cauliflower	Onion
Grape	Brussels sprout	Leek
	Squash	Pumpkin
	Endive	Potatoes

December

Fruits	Vegetables	
Kiwi	Garlic	Spinach
Tangerine	Beetroot	Lamb's lettuce
Orange	Carrot	Turnip
Grapefruit	Celery	Onion
Pear	Brussels sprout	Leek
Apple	Squash	Pumpkin
	Endive	Potatoes

Copyright © 2017
All rights reserved
Photo credit : Fotolia

Printed in Great Britain
by Amazon